# Is That A Rat On the Mat?

*Teaching Beginning Readers*

by

## VIOLA GRAYS-WILEY

# DEDICATION

This book is dedicated to the
Parents, Grandparents, Teachers,
And all who may be surrounded
By Early Learners.
*A Reading Jumpstart!*

The fat cat sat
all day looking
for one little rat.


Can you help her
find the rat?

"Is that a rat

on the mat?"

asked the cat.

# What is that?

I don't know
what is that,
but that is not a rat
on the
mat!

No, that is not

a rat on the mat.

That is a bear

sitting on the mat,

you silly cat!

"Is that a rat

on the mat?"

asked the cat.

# What is that?

I don't know
what is that,
but that is not a rat
on the
mat!

No, that is not

a rat on the mat.

That is a dog

sitting on the mat,

you silly cat!

"Is that a rat
on the mat?"
asked the cat.

# What is that?

I don't know
what is that,
but that is not a rat
on the
mat!

No, that is not

a rat on the mat.

That is a hat

sitting on the mat,

you silly cat!

"Is that a rat

on the mat?"

asked the cat.

11

# What is that?

I don't know
what is that,
but that is not a rat
on the
mat!

No, that is not
a rat on the mat.
That is a puppy
sitting on the mat,
you silly cat!

"Is that a rat

on the mat?"

asked the cat.

# What is that?

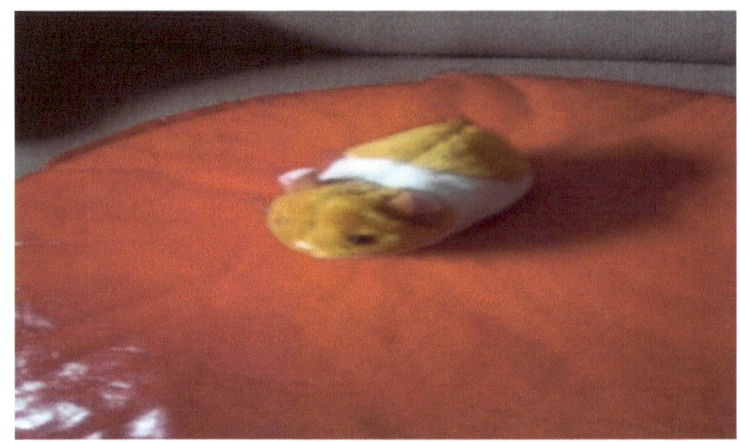

I don't know
what is that,
but that is not a rat
on the
mat!

No, that is not
a rat on the mat.

That is a hamster
sitting on the mat,
you silly cat!

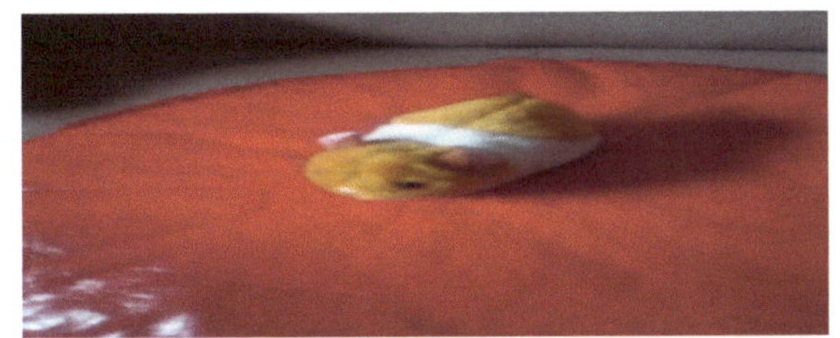

"Are those rats

with the mat?"

asked the cat.

No, those aren't rats with the mat.

Those are stuffed animals hiding the mat, you silly cat!

I am the rat looking for my mat. Did you see the fat cat with my red mat?

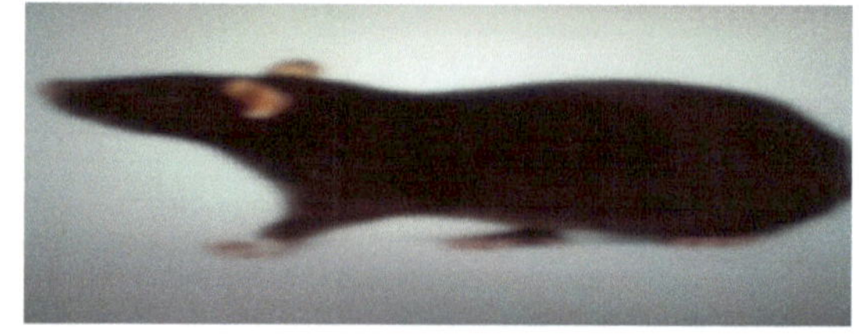

I don't want
to see
the fat cat
that took
my red mat!

The fat cat

took my

red mat,

so I ran away!

I don't want to
find that cat,
just my red mat
so I can
run and play.

Yes, I am the rat

who was on the

red mat,

when

the cat came

out to play!

Please help

*me* find my

red mat,

don't help

*the silly cat!*

Where is my mat!

So, I was the

rat who sat

on the mat,

and

that is that!

*Don't tell the cat*

*you saw me today!*

*I have an idea!*

## <u>Message</u>

## <u>To the Cat:</u>

*#matbegone*

*#ratbegone*

*#ratfindsnewmat*

# THE END